Rookie Read-About® Geography

Africa

by Rebecca Hirsch

Content Consultant
C. Gregory Knight
Geographer

Reading Consultant
Jeanne Clidas
Reading Specialist

Children's Press®
An Imprint of Scholastic Inc.
New York • Toronto • London • Auckland • Sydney • Mexico City
New Delhi • Hong Kong • Danbury, Connecticut

Library of Congress Cataloging-in-Publication Data
Hirsch, Rebecca E.
  Africa / by Rebecca Hirsch.
      p. cm. – (Rookie read-about geography)
  Includes index.
  ISBN 978-0-531-28975-4 (lib.bdg.) – ISBN 978-0-531-29275-4
(pbk.)
  1. Africa–Juvenile literature. 2. Africa–Geography–Juvenile
literature. I. Title.

DT12.25.H57 2012
960–dc23

                        2012013393

SCHOLASTIC, CHILDREN'S PRESS, ROOKIE READ-ABOUT®,
and associated logos are trademarks and/or registered trademarks of
Scholastic Inc.

18 19 20 R 25 24 23

Photos ©: cover: Gavin Hellier/Robert Harding Picture Library/age
fotostock; 4: Fernando Rodrigues/Dreamstime; 8: Kirk Treakle/Alamy
Images; 10: Ton Koene/age fotostock; 12: Ulrich Doering/age fotostock;
14: Marko5/Dreamstime; 16: Madd/Dreamstime; 18: WorldFoto/Alamy
Images; 20: Anthony Aneese Totah Jr./Dreamstime; 22: Metschurat/
Dreamstime; 24: Winfield Parks/National Geographic/Getty Images;
26: Paul Souders/WorldFoto; 28: John Warburton-Lee/Superstock, Inc.;
30: Peter Malsbury/iStockphoto; 31 top left: Marko5/Dreamstime; 31
top right: Anthony Aneese Totah Jr./Dreamstime; 31 bottom left: Paul
Souders/WorldFoto; 31 bottom right: Madd/Dreamstime.

Map by Matt Kania/Map Hero, Inc.

Scholastic Inc., 557 Broadway, New York, NY 10012.

Table of Contents

Buffalo drink at a watering hole.

Welcome to Africa!

Africa is a continent.
It has more than
50 countries.

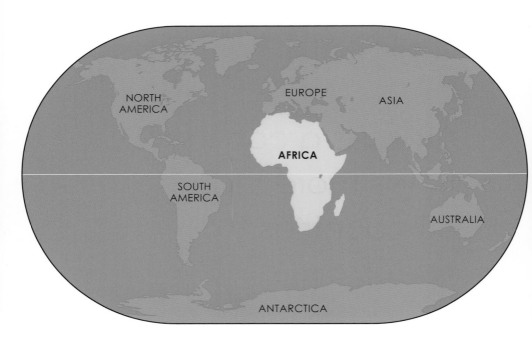

NORTH
AMERICA

EUROPE

ASIA

AFRICA

SOUTH
AMERICA

AUSTRALIA

ANTARCTICA

The largest pieces of land on Earth are continents. There are seven. Africa is the **yellow** continent on this map.

The Step Pyramid is near Cairo, Egypt.

People of Africa

Many people live in Africa. Some live in cities. Cairo is Africa's largest city. It is in Egypt. These children go to school near there.

A mother farms with her baby.

Some Africans work on farms. They grow corn, rice, and other crops.

Boys play on the beach
near Cape Town, South Africa.

Children play soccer in villages, cities, and on the beach. Soccer is the most popular sport in Africa.

Camels walk across the Sahara Desert.

Wild Places

Africa has deserts. The Sahara is the world's largest desert. It is very hot and dry.

Savannas have few trees.

Africa has grassy
places called
savannas. Savannas
have wet seasons and
dry seasons.

A national park rainforest in Africa

There are rainforests in Africa. It rains almost every day in the forest. Many kinds of plants grow there.

A silverback gorilla in the rainforest

Amazing Animals

Africa is famous for its wild animals. Gorillas live in the forest.

A herd of zebras

Zebras, giraffes, and lions live in the savanna.

Girls fill water jugs in the Nile River.

Water and Land

The Nile River in Africa is the world's longest river. People live near rivers so they can get water.

Kilimanjaro National Park in Africa

Kilimanjaro is Africa's tallest mountain. People climb this mountain. They visit Africa to see its amazing animals, people, and places.

Modern Marvels

- The Library of Alexandria in Africa is a very modern building.

- It has both sharp angles and smooth curves.

- Columns hold up the parts of the building.

- The Library of Alexandria can hold millions of books. It also has art galleries and museums.

Try It!

Can you find the rectangle shapes in this building? How many columns do you see? If you built a new library, what shape would you want it to be?

Meet a Meerkat

- Meerkats live together in family groups.

- Meerkat families work together to gather food and raise their young.

- You can find meerkats on the African savannas.

Words You Know

desert

gorilla

mountain

savanna

31

Index

Facts for Now

Visit this Scholastic Web site for more information on Africa:
www.factsfornow.scholastic.com
Enter the keyword **Africa**

About the Author

Rebecca Hirsch is a scientist-turned-writer and the author of many books for young readers.